little bit long time

ali cobby eckermann
little bit long time

PICARO PRESS

Acknowledgements

'I Tell You True' won First Prize at the inaugural
ATSI Survival Competition 2006.

'One Child Two Child Wailing and Wild' was shortlisted in
the Dymocks Red Earth Poetry Award
and printed in NT Literary Awards anthology 2007.

'Intervention Pay Back' won First Prize in
the Dymocks Red Earth Poetry Award, NT Literary Awards 2008.

little bit long time
ISBN 978 1 921691 76 8
Copyright © text Ali Cobby Eckermann 2015

This edition published 2017 by
Picaro Press – an imprint of
GINNINDERRA PRESS
PO Box 3461 Port Adelaide 5015 Australia
www.ginninderrapress.com.au

Contents

The Mountain	7
First Time (I Met My Grandmother)	8
One Child Two Child Wailing and Wild	9
Cloud Storm	10
Mother	12
Dingo Eye	13
Karen	14
Who?	16
A Dream	17
Circles and Squares	18
Untitled	20
Table Manners	21
2 Pelicans	22
How Does a Father Feel?	24
Kumana	25
Ribbons	26
Mum Said!	27
I Tell You True	28
Love Dreaming	29
Tears For Mum	30
Shrine	31
little bit long time	32
Emptiness	33
Too Afraid To Cry	34
Black	35
Intervention Payback	36
Messages	41

for Mum Frieda
a very special mother

and Mum Audrey
a very cherished friend

The Mountain

Lips crack
bleeding,

the mountain dries up
on my tongue.

Hands blister
clumsy,

the mountain rises up
on my fingers.

I sit to watch
and wait.

A bird comes.
I ask nothing

turn and grasp
the view.

First Time (I Met My Grandmother)

For Rosina

Sit down in the dirt and brush away the flies
Sit down in the dirt and avoid the many eyes

I never done no wrong to you, so why you look at me?
But if you gotta check me out, well go ahead – feel free!

I feel that magic thing you do, you crawl beneath my skin
To read the story of my Soul, to find out where I been

And now yous mob you make me wait, so I just sit and sit
English words seem useless, I know Language just a bit

I sit quiet way, not lonely, 'cos this country sings loud Songs
I never been out here before, but I feel like I belong

It's three days now, the mob comes back, big smiles are on their face
'This your Grandmother's Country here, this is your homeland place'

'We got a shock when we seen you, you got your Nana's face
We was real sad when she went missing in that cold Port Pirie place'

I understand the feelings now, tears push behind my eyes
I'll sit on this soil anytime, and brush away the flies

I'll dance with mob on this red Land, munda wiru place
I'll dance away them half caste lies 'cos I got my Nana's face!

One Child Two Child Wailing and Wild

Urgent darkness hunts us south, while my stomach churns with childbirth
He waits.

Foetal juices of blood and life baptise this child from my womb
He waits.

I wash my child with sand of red, avoid newborn eyes of trust
He waits.

A feeble cry escapes the grave. I watch it enter Heaven
He waits.

red band   black man
husband and father
gently   holds our toddler daughter
he has watched mine
now   I watch his back
survival dictates our nomadic trek

We walk silent strong in single-file fashion, stumble our way to the mission
He waits.

I bite and kick and scratch and scream "Don't take ***this*** child from me!"
He waits.

We sit broken together.
Darkness waits.

Cloud Storm

For Katie Allen

White and wispy   beards flap   in the sky majestic
    as the storm front approaches
        I stare at the wall of faces
            wise men   Unaipon   dead men
        handsome men   men with anguish
I see animals that accompany them   wild boar with razor tusks
                a panther cat buffalo and monkey.
            a symphony of colour storms behind
        amber and charcoal and fog floats rapidly toward me
        I see old Indians and other wati wrapped in furs
      wrinkled rippled cloud faces   I see my family
who have passed away and family patriarchs I never met
            slowly another shape emerges
        an eagle so large and so old   so frail yet
      so strong   I see into his cloud skin
        this totem being   the oldest wedgetail   in the world.
I notice the string of men   their anger and anguish   attached
are resting on the eagles wing   the wings stretched far.
his manner determined   he carries the storm of men on his feathers
            quickly passes overhead
behind the rolling drum of thunder and amber pastel pale floats kindness
    women of song   strong women of tremendous beauty
soft and happy supporting their men.

'Let them rage,' the women told me, 'because they have been wronged.'
      they whispered wind words in Kaurna and Kokatha
in Narrunga and Ngarandjeri the women told me, 'Let them rage.'

'Through where wrong began   where the grandparents were
kicked off the Land   given housing trust and heroin
and then kicked out of there   kicked out of the Square.'
'Let them rage,' they whispered   the women floated past   some smiled
some sang   some lay upon white furs and satin clouds
the feel of luxury I cannot describe   but their smiles above me did
the wind strengthened each heart beat   I saw white caps stream
as the wind from under the eagles wings moved across the water.
white tips of icing upon emerald green and royal blue
dust and sand blew in my eyes
closing them I breathed   I had waited
for that breath for weeks   maybe months
I turned to the direction of the city
I saw dust gather where oceans waters end
Dust ghosts formed   climbed on to the land   with huge steps
and hefty arms marched out of sight   to the city
the rain arrived
drums of thunder continued   wind blasted doubt off
my skin   and off my soul
I sit at the window and watch the rain   the wind and the white caps
I wonder about the men
I think of my son
Instantly   lightning flashes
Horizontally   a cheeky smile across the sky

Mother

Why can't you run to me
Hug me   hold me close
With the ferocity like kangaroos
Embraced in death like throes.

Dingo Eye

For Michelle and the kids

Serpentine Gorge is empty
shiny heat wave
shimmer

Birds have flown the billabong
frogs bury, dormant
wait for the next rain

I peer
into eyes of dingo

Airless, motionless
we hold that stare

The first moment
before breath expires
before understanding

A blink of my eye
the dingo vanishes
with fading dusk.

Karen

Mum said 'No school today'   Christopher and I didn't catch the bus
Even Dad stopped work on the farm that day.
We were going to Adelaide and wore our Sunday best
Although it wasn't.

Mum had shined the car   our yellow and white Vauxhall
With the rip in the front seat where the spring poked through.
Dad packed an empty bassinet with
White baby blankets and lace.

In Rundle Street we went to Coles cafeteria for lunch.

I felt very grown-up

Choosing my own food   carrying my own tray back to the table
Christopher and I had fish and chips with
Lots of salt and sauce.

Later we stopped at a house, a 'special place' Mum said
and walked inside.

Mum and Dad went up the corridor with a smiling lady
and James asleep on Dad's hip.

'Wait here' we were told. We waited a long time
Christopher and I sitting together.

Another lady came to tell us how lucky we are to belong
to such a special family.

She smiled a lot and seemed to know us
We didn't know who she was.

Mum and Dad and James came back into the room.
Asleep in the bassinet was a tiny baby
With yellow hair and tiny fingers curled in a fist.
Mum said 'Your sister's name is Karen.'

We drove with the baby back to the farm.
Mum was very excited
I let the baby's fingers curl around one of mine.
'That was a great shop' I thought to myself.

Who?

This poem is dedicated to my birth father

who I have never met

who I forgive.

A Dream

I saw you dance
that summer
before the war.
Your face
painted,
proudly celebrates
your hunting skills.

Women
in awe, whisper
behind their hands
of your strength
and bravery.

The headdress
you wear
reflects
your rightful place
of leadership
and wisdom.

This was
before
the white man came

and murdered you.

Circles and Squares

I was born yankunytjatjara my mother is yankunytjatjara her mother was yankunytjatjara my family is yankunytjatjara I have learnt many things from my family elders I have grown to recognise that life travels in circles aboriginal culture has taught me this

When I was born I was not allowed to live with my family I grew up in the white man's world

We lived in a square house we picked fruit and vegetables from a neat fenced square plot
we kept animals in square paddocks we ate at a square table we sat on square chairs
I slept in a square bed

I looked at myself in a square mirror and did not know who I was

One day I met my mother

I began to travel I visited places that I had already been but this time I sat down with family

We gathered closely together by big round campfires we ate bush tucker feasting on round ants and berries we ate meat from animals that live in round burrows we slept in circles on beaches around our fires we sat in the dirt on our land that belongs to a big round planet
we watched the moon grow to a magnificent yellow circle that was our time

I have learnt two different ways now I am thankful for this that is part of my Life Circle

My heart is Round ready to echo the music of my family but the Square within me remains

The Square stops me in my entirety.

Untitled

The pink
and grey
galah lies
dead
on the bitumen.

Grey bitumen
lies
dead
under galah
pink sky.

Table Manners

For Kate Lawrence

Warrior woman walks proudly
Close to where I sit in the street.
I notice her mute smile buried under scars.
Our eyes meet.

I bow my head.
'Sorry sis,' I say quietly, 'I got nothing.'
My friend looks at me, searches through her bag
'I might have something.'

I respect the warrior woman, ask 'What's your name?'
Her eyes are focused behind me.
Focused on another place
Along Todd Mall.

Suddenly her focus is at my shoulder,
'We told you before' waitress **yells** in my ear.
'You have to leave'
'You can't ask for money here.'

Warrior woman walks proudly
Away from where I sit today.
Her scarred face turns, smiles with her words –
'She's just jealous!'

2 Pelicans

For Harold and Mel

My friend was at the A & E, he wasn't feeling good
I was at the barbecue, just like he said I should.
The phone call from the hospital shocks me with fear and fright –
'You better come to ICU, he might not make it through the night.'

I stand silent at his bedside, he looks so dead already,
I try comforting his children as their lives become unsteady.
'Please don't go away' I whisper 'don't leave us behind.'
I pray then to my Ancestors, I ask them for a sign.

We sit all night like statues, on each side of his bed,
The thought of losing him is really fucking with my head!
The nursing staff fuss round with looks of deep regret.
But I was waiting for a sign that he won't leave us yet.

The morning light creeps slowly across red desert sand
His eyelids flicker open and he fumbles for my hand.
'Hello' he whispers 'how are you?' and then falls back to sleep
My eyes stare at the monitors, the bips, the dots, the beeps.

'He's out of danger' the doctor says 'you should get some rest.'
And as I walked along Gap Road I look out to the west
2 pelicans fly overhead, floating on the breeze,
'It's the sign' I cry and thank the Spirits watching over me.

I return to the hospital, he is much stronger now
And the nursing staff all smiling as they too wonder how?
I share the story of the sign, the pelicans in the sky
We hold each others hands and smiles are in our eyes.

I drive out to Amoonguna to tell family he is right
I sit down with his Aunty, round the campfire, in the night
I ask her to explain the pelicans and the meaning of the sign
She laughs and whispers 'Arrangkwe just 2 pelicans in the sky!'

How Does a Father Feel?

How does a father feel
After his child is abused?

Does he want to kill the man
Who stole innocence forever?

Does he want to sit alone
And hide, pretend, whatever?

Does he want to hit his wife
When her crying goes on and on?

Does he want to go drinking
With his mates, even that one?

What does a father feel
After his child is abused?

Kill hide hit deny
Speak to the man, even that one.

Kumana

For all my family in Port Augusta
in memory of brother R

There is no life
but Family.

When I am young
I live with my Family.

When I grow up
I leave my Family.

When I am lonely
I miss my Family.

When I am drunk
I reverse-charge my Family.

When I pass away
I unite my Family.

There is no life
but Family.

Ribbons

For minya Audrey and Merlin

'See you' I said to the children
as I memorised
their Anangu faces
filled with laughter
and trust for family
innocent in their youth
and strong in culture

'See you' I said to the Elders
as the tears flow
in my heart
and I bend down
to shake their hands
and gain my strength
by skin

'See you' I said at Murputja
and the dust from my car
as I drove away
was like a ribbon
across the desert sand
tying me to that place
forever

Mum Said!

Mum said she
wanted to give me a hug this morning
for all the smacks she gave me when I was a child
Mum said she
used to get so angry
Mum said she
struggled that I was different from other children
Mum said she
didn't know what to do back then
Mum said she
hoped I could forgive her.

She held open her arms
This adopted mother of mine
This woman with white skin   and white hair   and white heart.

I climb inside the embrace
This adopted daughter of hers
This woman with brown skin   and brown hair   and brown heart.

I said Mum
I forgave you a long time ago.

I Tell You True

I can't stop drinking, I tell you true
Since I watched my daughter perish
She burned to death inside a car
I lost what I most cherish
I saw the angels hold her
As I screamed with useless hope
I can't stop drinking, I tell you true
It's the only way I cope!

I can't stop drinking, I tell you true
Since I found my sister dead
She hung herself to stop the rapes
I found her in the shed
The rapist bastard still lives here
Unpunished in this town
I can't stop drinking, I tell you true
Since I cut her down.

I can't stop drinking, I tell you true
Since my mother passed away.
They found her battered down the creek
I miss her more each day
My family blamed me for her death
Their words have made me wild
I can't stop drinking, I tell you true
'Cos I was just a child.

So if you see someone like me
Who's drunk and loud and cursing
Don't judge too hard, you never know
What sorrows we are nursing.

Love Dreaming

When you went back to the waterhole
and sat under the mulberry tree
at the Ooldea soakage
did you see Daisy Bates
dressed in English attire
standing on the white sand dunes?

When you went back to the waterhole
and scooped the precious water
from the sandy sanctuary
did you hear the warriors
dancing in the moonlight
Snake and Emu making love?

When you go to the waterhole
do the white sand dunes
make love to the moonlight?
does the mulberry tree
scoop the precious water?
does Daisy hear the warriors
coming back, coming back.

Tears For Mum

Mum can I cry at your funeral, can I wail
Like I do out bush, can I walk the aisle in ochre
Can you tell the other kids that this is okay, this is
What I need, the way we grieve, proper way out bush

Mum can you explain that I need my sisters from Yuendumu
And Haasts Bluff by my side at your funeral
Can you tell the other kids that this is okay, this is
What I need, the way we grieve, proper way out bush

Mum can you understand this is the only way I know
To mend my aching heart when you pass away
Can you tell the other kids that this is okay, this is
What I need, the way we grieve, proper way out bush

Shrine

For Valerie Martin

Among the rubble
I prop a roof
from battered rusty tin
sunlight sparkles through

old nail holes
as will stars
and droplets
of refreshing rain.

I weight every stone
in my gaze
in my hands
I sweep

earthen floor
remove impurities
from its skin as
it has done mine.

I gaze at
clouded glass
no longer.

little bit long time

For all our old mob who told us true

'Stay here'
he whispers gruffly   holds her roughly
hugs her   then hides her
little bit long time.

Big eyes young face   stare from hiding place
watch her Dad pause   check nature's laws
sniffing the air   eyes filled with despair
little bit long time.

He just wants some water   to give to his daughter
he steps from the trees   crawls on his knees
squats in the sand   drinks with his hands
little bit long time.

Her eyes do not waver   good lessons he gave her
sees Dad fall over strange   there a hole in his brains
gun noise fills her ears   her eyes lose their tears
little bit long time.

Rough white hands snatch her   cruel voices scratch her
she's too scared to run   she's learnt respect for the gun
two different eyes clash   she knows in a flash
this killer had watched them

little bit long time.

Emptiness

The big black bird struts proud
defiantly
along my front fence garden.
'Fark' it screeches loud.

The whole street can hear
yet no movement
no one walking around
no friendship
no sense of community.

A knock at the window
I look out quickly.
The branch bangs on the glass again,
the breeze blows by.
An empty beer can rattles,
rolls along the empty street.

The big black bird struts proud
defiantly
along my front fence garden.
'Fark' it screeches loud.

I sit inside
thinking exactly the same thing.

Too Afraid To Cry

For my most precious son Jonnie

red-skimpy-top-and-denim-skirt
enters the hotel   no body attached
nervous   glances ricochet
scuttle into awkward   silence

loud barracking of
Friday night fever erupts
red-skimpy-and-denim drinks
jostled   in testosterone crowd
enjoys cold frothy beer

a stupor of numbness
saturates her clothes
an alcoholic grin appears
skimpy-denim drinks
desolate   fear   hatred
short-denim-skirt-and-skimpy-top
begins to float away

the infant face of my son
kissed goodbye
slashes through my
core   my heart
too afraid to cry

I gaze down at my body
I am wearing
a denim skirt and red skimpy top

Black

For Mum Audrey, a true activist

1

My father is a unicorn
The mythical beast
Hidden behind clouds
Of gossip.

My mother grasps curtains
Shreds them with anxiety
Plaits ribbons
In an empty church.

My nana opens windows
Weaving songs
And gently tells
Real myths.

2

My father thinks I am not his

My mother thinks she knows me

My nana thinks I am her heart

But I am none of these

I am white
I am grey
I am black.

Intervention Payback

I love my wife   she right skin for me   pretty one my wife young one   found her at the next community over   across the hills   little bit long way   not far

and from there she give me good kids   funny kids mine   we always laughing   all together   and that wife   she real good mother   make our wali real nice   flowers and grass patch and chickens   I like staying home with my kids

and from there I build cubby house   yard for the horse   see I make them things from left overs   from the dump   all the left overs from fixing the houses   and all the left overs I build cubby house and chicken house

and in the house we teach the kids   don't make mess   go to school learn good so you can work round here later   good job good life   and the government will leave you alone

and from there tjamu and nana tell them the story   when the government was worse rations   government make u[all the rules   but don't know culture   can't sit in the sand   oh tjamu and nana   they got the best story   we always laughing us mob

and from there night time when we all asleep   all together on the grass patch   dog and cat and kids   my wife and me them kids they ask really good questions about the olden days about today   them real ninti them kids   they gunna be right and from there come intervention   John Howard   he make new rules   he never even come to see us   how good we was doing already   Mal Brough   he come with the army   we got real frightened true   thought he was gonna take the kids away   just like tjamu and nana bin tell us

I run my kids in the sand hills   took my rifle up there and sat   but they was all just lying   changing their words all the time   wanting meeting today   and meeting tomorrow   we was getting sick of looking at them   so everyone put their eyes down   and some even shut their ears

and from there I didn't care too much   just kept working fixing the housing   being happy working hard   kids go to school   wife working hard too   didn't care too much   we was right   we always laughing us mob   all together

but then my wife she come home crying   says the money in quarantine but I didn't know why they do that   we was happy not drinking and fighting   why they do that we ask the council to *stop the drinking and protect the children*   hey you know me ya bloody mongrel I don't drink   and I look after my kids   I bloody fight ya you say that again   *hey settle down we not saying that   Mal Brough saying that   don't you watch the television   he making the rules for all the mobs   every place Northern Territory he real cheeky whitefella   but he's the boss   we gotta do it*

and from there I tell my wife she gets paid half half in hand
half in the store   her money in the store now   half and half
me too   all us building mob   but I can't buy tobacco   or
work boots   you only get the meat and bread   just like the
mission days   just like tjamu and nana tell us

and from there I went to the store to get meat for our supper
but the store run out   only tin food left   so I asked for some
bullets   I'll go shoot my own meat   but sorry they said
you gotta buy food   that night I slept hungry   and I slept
by myself   thinking about it

and from there the government told us our job was finish   the
government been give us the sack   we couldn't believe it   we
been working CDEP   for years   slow way park the truck at the
shed   just waiting   for something   for someone with tobacco

the other men's reckon   fuck this   drive to town for the grog
but I stayed with my kids   started watching the television
trying to laugh   not to worry   just to be like yesterday

and from there the politician man says *I give you real job* tells
me to work again   but different   only half time sixteen hours
but I couldn't understand   it was the same job as before   but
more little   less pay   and my kids can't understand   when
they come home from school   why I cant buy the lolly for
them like I used to before   I didn't want to tell them   I get
less money for us now

and from there they say   my wife earns too much money   I gonna miss out again   I'm getting sick of it   don't worry she says   I'll look after you   but I know that's not right way I'm getting shame   my brother   he shame too   he goes to town drinking   leaves his wife behind   leaves his kids

and from there I drive round to see tjamu   he says his money in the store too   poor bloke   he can't even walk that far and I don't smile   I look at the old man   he lost his smile too   but nana she cook the damper and tail   she trying to smile   she always like that

and from there when I get home   my wife gone to town with the sister in law   she gone look for my brother   he might be stupid on the grog   he not used to it   she gotta find him   might catch him with another woman   make him bleed   drag him home

and from there my wife   she come back   real quiet   tells me she went to casino   them others took her   taught her the machines   she lost all the money   she lost her laughing

and from there all the kids bin watching us   quiet way   not laughing around   so we all go swimming down the creek all the families there together   we happy again   them boys we take them shooting   chasing the malu in the car   we real careful with the gun   not gonna hurt my kids   no way

and from there my wife   she sorry   she back working hard
save the money   kids gonna get new clothes   I gonna get
my tobacco and them bullets   but she gone change again
getting her pay   forgetting her family   forget yesterday
only thinking for town   with the sister in law

and my wife   she got real smart now   drive for miles all
dressed up   going to the casino with them other kungkas   for
the Wednesday night draw

I ready told you I love my kids   I only got five   two pass
away already   and I not complaining bout looking after my
kids   no way   but when my wife gets home   if she spent
all the money   not gonna share with me and the kids

I might hit her   first time

wali – house
tjamu – grandfather
ninti – clever
malu – kangaroo
kungkas – women

Messages

For Nana Myra Watson and Aunty Nura Ward

Every grain of sand in this
big red country
is a pore on the skin
of my Family

Every feather on the ground in this
spinifex country
is a spiritual message
from my Ancestors.

Every wild flower that blooms in this
desert of red
is a signpost of hope
for my People.

www.ingramcontent.com/pod-product-compliance
Lightning Source LLC
Chambersburg PA
CBHW071040080526
44587CB00015B/2702